History of Abortion Law

Abortion itself is an ancient practice, so ancient that no one really knows when or where it was first performed. The Hippocratic oath is a significant Greek reference that contains condemnation of abortion.

In English common law the thirteenth century English jurist Henry Bracton discussed that life actually begins at the moment of quickening rather than a given number of days after conception, killing the fetus after the occurrence of the quickening was murder, whereas before that time it was no crime." If there be someone, who has struck a pregnant woman, or has given her poison, whereby he has caused abortion, if the foetus be already formed and animated, and particularly if it be animated, he commits homicide."(Quay, Justifiable Abortion-Medical and Legal Foundations, 49 Geo. L. J. 395)

For all practical purposes, until 1803, abortion was primarily a religious offense, punishable by such sanctions as the Church was able to impose.

Issues such as abortion and birth-control are even more political than ever before.

The recent discussion of abortion is now mostly divided into two sides, pro-life and pro- choice, being now considered a fundamental women's right visible in politics, media, and culture. Abortion and reproductive health are now a major issues in politics.

Abortion discourse has also been about what is the time that a fetus makes the transition from a living being to a living human being. In religion, this issue is generally conceptualized in terms of when the fetus embodies a soul.

Abortion is very common in the US. 1 out of 3 women go through an abortion before they reach 45 .

The most powerful opposition to abortion came from the church. Abortion was denounced, for example, in the first known Christian writings. It was labeled "murder by way of advance" by Tertullian (155-222 A.D.). Before Trump was elected, the Supreme Court did not have the five pro-choice votes needed to overturn the decision, but with his opportunity to choose two Supreme Court seats there has been a race to create restrictive abortion bills so that they can pass while Republicans have the majority.

According to The New York Times, nine states have passed bills on abortion that "challenge the constitutional right established in Roe v. Wade." (Lai: n.p.).

In Alabama, a law was passed declaring that abortion is only legal if the mother's life is at risk or the fetus cannot survive, and Louisiana passed a bill where abortion is only allowed until the first heartbeat.

In the USA, abortion was legal for a long time before the quickening period that when a person starts feeling the movement of the fetus. Till the 1800s all procedures use for abortion were highly risky. There were very limited hospitals in the USA with no concept of antiseptic.

The preliminary medical education wasn't enough to perform successful surgeries. Even the death rate of children and mothers during childbirth was extremely high so abortion was even more dangerous for mothers too.

In response to proliferation, mid-19th-century abortion was criminalized. Initially, this anti-abortion law was a poison control measure that was common at that time. Late 19th century many states started banning abortion laws except to save the life of a pregnant woman. The Ban of abortion was for many reasons as initially, it was against the movement of women's right to voluntary motherhood. This law was made to control women and confine them to the only childbearing role. Another reason for banning abortion was because of high catholic immigrants. The birth rate of these immigrants was much higher than the local women. The US government and agencies were worried about race suicide so they wanted white protestant women to have more babies [2]. This race discrimination supported the abortion ban.

The Struggle of Illegal Abortion

Although at the end of the 19th-century medical surgeries were becoming safer for abortion still women were not allowed to go for abortions. Women left with no choice than going for illegal abortion which put a heavy toll on their health, mental stress, and finance. This illegal abortion era started the most dangerous "black alley abortions".

Moreover, sex outside of the marriage institution was not socially sanctioned and women saw abortion as a way to escape stigma if they were pregnant. Abortion and sometimes infanticide were often a result of female desperation.

Either women have had to travel abroad to find a physician for safe abortion or to rely on incompetent midwives. Women with resources still have the choice for safe surgeries while flying out. For self-inducing abortion, women started inserting knitting needles or coat hangers into the vagina and uterus douched with hard chemicals.

These types of self-induction abortions caused many life causalities and many women were left with severe illness, chronic pain, or infertility. As these deaths were not officially reported, so it's unknown the exact number of deaths caused by illegal abortions. Chicago's public hospital named Cook Country Hospital has one ward for women suffering from an illegal abortion. That ward remained full of suffering women.

1) https://www.guttmacher.org/news-release/2017/abortion-common-experience-us-women-despite-dramatic-declines-rates
2). https://www.ourbodiesourselves.org/book-excerpts/health-article/u-s-abortion-history/

Making Illegal Abortion Safer For Women

In the illegalization of abortion, many people struggled to help a woman for safe abortion. In 1960, a network [Clergy Consultation Service](#) supported illegal abortion with inexpensive and safe abortions. In 1969 Abortion Counseling Service of the Chicago Women's Liberation Union provided 11,000 safe abortions in 4 years with safety levels to today's legal medical facility. Between 1967 and 1973, 14 states reformed and 4 replaced the restrictive law of abortion especially when pregnancy was the result of rape or incest [2].

The US Supreme Court

All the events discussed earlier were favoring legislation of abortion because many women were dying for opting for unsafe options. Women's life safety and the political will of overlapping women's movements were the main reason to legalize abortion.

On 22 January 1973, Supreme Court landmark Roe v. Wade legalized abortion 1973 by stating people have a right to privacy against the state interest in maternal health and fetal life. It stated abortion is legal till it's done by a registered physician [2].

As the pregnancy is divided into 3 trimesters, the choice of abortion will rely on the trimester. The decision of abortion in 1st trimester will rely on pregnant women on the consultation of the doctor. The state may interfere the abortion in 2nd trimester for maternal health. In 3rd trimester, the state may prohibit abortion as per the life and health concerns of the mother and the baby. If the abortion is performed after the third month of pregnancy, a miniature caesarean operation, is performed. This process requires an incision in the lower abdomen, through which the fetus is removed.

Although Roe V Wade didn't settle the abortion issue completely still his statement appeared as a benchmark in the abortion law 1973. When the Supreme Court's decisions go against the values and preferences of a considerable portion of the public in a state or region, implementation may be a difficult, lengthy, and expensive process.

United States Supreme Court ruled in Roe v. Wade (410 U.S. 113) that access to abortion during the first three months of pregnancy was guaranteed by Constitutional provisions concerning privacy. But the Court's action did not remove the controversial question of abortion from the public to the private domain. Instead, Roe has contributed to continuing public debate over the implications of abortion for welfare policy, civil liberties, race relations, religion, and women's rights.

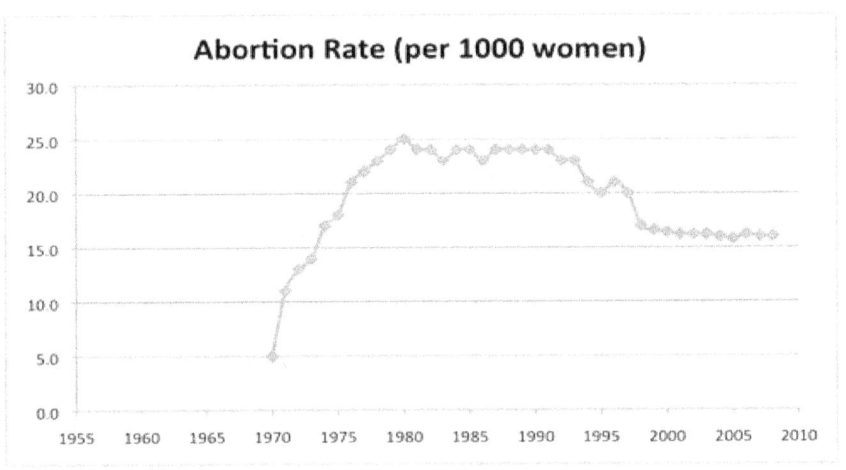

The chart [3] shows the huge increase in abortion after the statement of Roe V Wade to legalize abortion. A level off was observed for a long time. After 1995

a huge decrease in abortion has been seen across the US because of the availability and use of contraceptive medicines. After the regime of Roe v. Wade, the government started providing legal abortion access.

3) http://www.cdc.gov/Reproductivehealth/Data_Stats/#Abortion

In 1976 Congress made the first Hyde amendment [4] to use the funds of federal Medicaid to provide legal abortion services to all women. Some legalization authorities protested that the public should not give taxes to support abortion while denying the fact that abortion is the basic right of a woman to choose for their life.

Guttmacher institute found at that time women with resources have the choice to go for safe abortion while 35% of women with a low income had no choice. Either poor women go for incompetent midwives or self-inducing abortions because of no public funds. So the availability of funds for abortion was made to ensure the life of all women.

Roe v Wade

Even during the time of Roe v Wade many hard-core catholic were protesting and raising their voice against abortion. In 1976 first arson [5] happened when a group of people started a peaceful protest outside an abortion clinic. The protesting crowd blocked the entrance of the clinic and tried to stop women to enter and started threatening clinical staff to perform an abortion. Anti-abortion ideologies keep protesting with more horrible tactics as bombing and the use of dangerous chemicals to stop women to get aborted.

- Before the 1980s the abortion laws were strongly linked to the women's rights movement and has no link with any political party. But after 1980, the Republican Party ended its 40-year commitment [6] with the Equal Rights Amendment (ERA). ERA was a proposed amendment for equal rights for women. In the meanwhile, President Reagan appointed some anti-abortion judges in the Supreme Court. Since then political landscape is more divided because of abortion laws.

- *Webster v. Reproductive Health Services* (1989) and *Planned Parenthood v. Casey* (1992) placed more limits on women's abilities to get an abortion
- In February 1980, the Supreme Court struck down congressional
- restrictions on Medicaid abortions pending full Court review

Opposition against abortion laws was raising in the different parts of the country and even some states were making their law strict against abortion. From 1989 to 1992, 700 restrictions were made in the state legalization of abortion law. In 2000, the new medicine mifepristone was introduced. It was used for nonsurgical abortion care and was also authorized by FDA as safe medicine [7]. By 2005, about one-fifth of women received an abortion through this medicine. Still, many politicians opposed the availability of this mifepristone.

The current debate over legal issues, funding formulas, and administrative discretion has resulted in frequent policy changes which cause confusion amongst people.

TEXAS HEsARTBEAT LAW

From Wednesday 1 September, Gov. Greg Abbott signed a law to ban abortion after six weeks of pregnancy [8]. This law bans abortion when the fetus starts its heartbeat and even before a woman realized that she is pregnant. As per a report earlier, 80- 90% of abortions happen after 6 weeks so most clinics will get close now. Government will grant the citizen the right to sue the doctor performing termination after the cut-off mark.

4) Rose M. *Abortion*. Westport, Connecticut: Greenwood publishing group. 2008

5) http://www.prochoice.org/about_abortion/violence/history_violence.html

6). Hout M. Abortion politics in the United States, 1972-1994: From single issue to ideology. *Gender Issues*. 1999;17(2):3-34

7) https://www.fda.gov/drugs/postmarket-drug-safety-information-patients-and-providers/mifeprex-mifepristone-information

8) https://www.texastribune.org/2021/05/18/texas-heartbeat-bill-abortions-law/

In the Law signing ceremony, Greg Abbott said "our Creator has gifted us with life but many children lose the right of life because of abortion. Let's agree to support a bill that I am to sign that ensures that the life of every unborn child has a heartbeat, matter and will be saved from the damage of abortion".

This law also ensures the ban on abortion in case of rape and incest while only have exceptions for medical emergencies.

Many states of the USA have passed anti-abortion bills but the Texas bill is different. Texas bill empowers citizens to sue the doctor or anyone who helps in the abortion after the first fetal heartbeat is detected. As per law people who sue the doctor will get the award of 10,000 $ with the cost of attorney if they win [9].

As per statistics, more than 619,591 abortions reported in 2018 from all states in the USA. So, by this law, the government could save the lives of 619,591 children by next year. Restrictions and advancements in the availability of abortion have come in waves, in recent years, there seem to be two of these waves happening simultaneously some states moving forward with stricter abortion laws and blue states improving its accessibility.

9) https://www.texastribune.org/2021/05/18/texas-heartbeat-bill-abortions-law/
10) https://www.cdc.gov/mmwr/volumes/69/ss/ss6907a1.htm

GLOBAL ABORTION LAWS

Although abortion law varies across the world as per region and its religions and culture, in most countries, abortion is legal under some circumstances of women's health, rape, and incest. Around the globe six countries El Salvador, Malta, Chile, the Dominican Republic, the Vatican, and Nicaragua abortion is banned with no exception. It means in any case of rape or incest or even fetus abnormality a woman has to bring a pregnancy to its end term. 125 countries provide abortion on special request to save women's health, socioeconomic condition, and risk of woman physical or mental health or in case of fetal anomalies.

11) https://maps.reproductiverights.org/worldabortionlaws

Abortion Leads to Demographic Disturbances

China legalized abortion in 1950 and promoted a 1 child per family policy [12].

China enacted the law of only 1 child in 1979 to control the population. This law came with severe restrictions including fines, compulsory abortion, and sterilization. This policy disturbed the demographic of the country as people start opting for abortion after gender revelation. The majority of people will go for an abortion in case of having a daughter.

In 2016 government raised the abortion law and start promoting 2 children per family. On 31 May 2021 China allowed 3 children per couple because statistic shows a decline in the birth rate [13]. There is also a chance that because of disturbing demographics, government and agencies could take coercive steps to restrict women from abortion in the future.

Data from the 1989-99 nation family health survey showed that the selection of gender is the main reason behind the abortion in Indian people which turns a heavy toll on demographic balance. The northern comparison shows that women are more literate, participate in labor and have a low preference for the boy. But in Southern India literacy rate is low and labor is needed for agriculture so people go for boy selection [14].

The government has decided now after a certain gestation limit of 20 weeks, that it's the doctor, not the mother who will decide either to terminate the pregnancy or not.

12) https://www.britannica.com/topic/one-child-policy
13) https://www.bbc.com/news/world-asia-china-57303592
14) https://www.thelancet.com/journals/langlo/article/PIIS2214-109X(21)00094-2/fulltext

Pro-Choice Vs Pro-Life

Pro-choice is the group of people that consider that it's a woman's chooses to get abort or not. Pro-life claims that every life, including the unborn child, has a right to live.

Pro-Choice

Pro-choice people are mostly feminist movement supporters. Many feminists started to demand birth control programs and sexual education as a way to boost women. The birth control movement became an important issue of the Women's Movement.

In the United States that ,Comstock Act in late 19th century prohibited the circulation of obscene material through the postal service, including information about contraceptives. By the 20th century feminists were calling for easy access and information about contraceptives both for middle class women and working class women.

In the 1840's, a patent for a diaphragm under the name "The Wife's Protector" was introduced in the United States. With time the use of contraceptives became widespread, but it continued to be a taboo well into the 20th century. In 1920s and 30s birth control became increasingly more socially accepted as working class women campaigned to legalize birth control and make education on it widespread.

By the 1960s the Supreme Court ruled that married couples had the right to use birth control, the pill was approved by the Food and Drug Organization (FDA).

The feminist movement in the 1960s, later labeled Second-Wave feminism, tried to decriminalize abortions and changed their focus to women's right to their bodies.

The pro-choice argument is that pregnancy is a woman's choice as it brings a lot of changes in her body and life. Pro-choice claims that the fetus is not a human being while in the womb. Therefore the rights of the fetus will not be the same as the human being and terminating pregnancy will not be counted as murder.

They argue that botched illegal abortions threaten the life of the mother. Most illegal abortions are not accompanied by the use of antibiotics and infections frequently follow.

Institutional policies that can restrict access to information about, prevent referrals to and deny treatment for essential reproductive healthcare services impact the entire community and make the prevention work of public health difficult, if not impossible.

The majority of healthcare organizations require employees to sign a statement of faith for employment and do not allow them to share information about family planning with consumers.

There are also gatekeepers at government and non-religious organizations that use their positions to restrict access to services. Department of Human Services staff was criticized for not allowing free condom distribution among items available to families in need. Similarly it was found out that unemployment agency denied information about family planning for the uninsured.

These denials of care disproportionately affect those who are the most disenfranchised and have the least access to healthcare. They are also impossible to enforce or monitor.

Because everyone has personal biases, health and human service providers can act in ways that make already existing inequalities worse. This is the result of restrictions in healthcare. Doctors deserve to be exposed to gender thinking and trainings.

The pro-choice argument is that denying the availability of a legal abortion is to force the religious and moral precepts of society upon women.

The proponents also argue that Pregnancy also limits the education and job opportunity for women. Raising many children or having unwanted babies will ruin women's health and children will ultimately suffer from neglect that will cost their whole life performance. Adoption is a choice that many women make while others believe that a woman goes through a lot in the procedure of pregnancy and labor that puts enough stress on her mental and physical health. So, they feel that a woman has a right to choose whether she wants to abort her child or not.

Pro-choice people also hold the view that the father is not held responsible by the state and only the mother suffers in case of an unwanted pregnancy.

There is a lack of sympathy for an unfortunate woman while 'the father of the child-even if proven of paternity" remains free of blame and burden and continues his life as respected member of society.

They argue the Abortion ban should have been bundled with mandatory vasectomy, mandatory childcare and financial support from the father; Because as humans we have the responsibility to protect our ecosystem.

Pro-Life Arguments

The position taken by nearly every opponent of legalized abortion is that the fetus is also a human being and, as such, has a right to life. They assert that no matter how high the rate of maternal death or how great the risk of harm is with illegal abortions, the mortality rate of the unborn children is 100 percent.

Most pro-life people are religious and emphasize fetus rights. Pro-life supports the bible verse "Thou shalt not kill".

The Catholic Church opposes abortion in all circumstances and often leads the national debate on abortion. Religious Exemption Laws Allow health care providers, like hospitals, doctors, nurses, clinics, and health insurance companies, to refuse to treat a woman seeking an abortion.

Pro-life people argue that Abortion by definition is the ending of a life. It is an elective procedure. By definition it destroys life. By no means is it an essential procedure. There are multiple ways to prevent a pregnancy. People having sex would know how to prevent pregnancy. Women rights should not be used as an excuse to end the life of her child because it's convenient. This would be not just self-centered but cruel to the small new life growing the womb.

One of the key issues in relation to abortion law is the determination of the legal status of the fetus; is it simply a mass of tissue, basically only a part of the mother, merely a potential person?

"If the personhood of the unborn can be established as a matter of law, then such 'persons' would be entitled to the same right to life as born individuals".

A newborn infant is not a great deal more personlike than a nine month fetus, and thus it might seem that if late-term abortion is sometimes justified, then infanticide must also be sometimes justified. Yet most people consider that infanticide is a form of murder, and thus never justified.

The pro-life debate also emphasizes that abortion is nihilistic. They prefer meaninglessness and choose to end life in an thoughtful manner.

They argue that "mental illness" is an excuse to end unplanned pregnancy. There are complex issues that lead women to abortion that lead her further into mental illness. This mental distress is no surprise as the loss of a child, especially at your own will, is a completely human response to have. Mental illness follows because it's very inhumane to kill your own offspring.

A fetus is a human life a live person. In recent years, when people were asked if abortion was morally wrong, almost half of Americans said that it was (47 percent), with only 13 percent reporting that abortion was morally acceptable, and 27 percent stating that abortion is not a moral issue, according to Pew Research Centre. Larger percentages of Protestants and Catholics reported believing abortion to be morally wrong (56 and 58 percent) and only 20 percent of those without an affiliation held this belief. ([The Pew Forum on Religion and Public Life, 2013b](#)).

The increased use of contraceptives, improvements in consistency of use and greater reliance on highly effective methods can reduce levels of unintended pregnancy.

According to an analysis of data from the 2006–2010 National Survey of Family Growth, long-acting reversible xontraceptive (LARC) methods have begun to displace shorter term methods among women using contraceptives, especially those younger than 25, who are traditionally at high risk of unintended pregnancy. (Finer LB, Jerman J and Kavanaugh ML, Changes in use of longacting contraceptive methods in the United States, 2007–2009, Fertility and Sterility, 2012, 98(4):893–897.)

Religion Abortion and the State

Religion and abortion are closely connected in political and social discourse in the United States. Most major religions express doctrinal disapproval of abortion.

Another cause is the religious and social ostracism placed upon illegitimate conception. It is fairly recent that the American society has shown any acceptance for illegal conception.

The pro –life people assert that it is in the interest of a State to protect the fetus, based on the concept of "morality" or "natural law," in addition to religious codes. They claim that feticide violates of the basic code of conduct of societal norms based on religion and otherwise.

Some social philosophers argue that man is not merely a chemical machine and that he possesses a soul from the earliest stages of fetal development. Therefore the fetus cannot be destroyed.

Most moral values (even those of atheists) stem from Abrahamic religions, and only degenerate understandings of these religions allow people to become a moral police and play god.

Deeper readings would always warn people to avoid these tendencies at all costs. But the idea that religion and politics are separate, mutually exclusive domains is actually very modern and very Western. Of course being modern and Western is not problematic, but to take a modern Western idea and universalize it as an irrefutable fact true for ever and for all is grossly wrong.

Various religious, medical, psychological, and legal organizations have been striving to reach some level of accord on the issues involved in promulgating a realistic and acceptable policy toward abortion. Most civilizations of antiquity prohibited the practice of abortion. Ancient Judaism prohibited birth control except in times of famine. Assyrian law imposed the death penalty upon any person participating in an abortion, including the procurer.

I will not go into the history of European politics to explain how and why religion and politics broke apart, but it is enough to say that it was the corruption and abuse of religion for political purposes that led to secularization in the West.

The problem therefore is the abuse of religion for power, not the religious state itself. Therefore, to believe that the secular state is the ideal for progressive societies whereas religious states are regressive, backward and intolerant is a completely false, Eurocentric idea. It is not as simple as that. Karen Armstrong considers the idea of the Secular state to be an anomaly and an aberration from the collective human experience.

Abortion is not an isolated moral issue; to fully understand the moral status of abortion we may have to reconsider other moral issues as well, issues not just about infanticide and euthanasia, but also about the moral rights of women and of nonhuman animals.

We can read Uday Mehta's work, called Liberalism and Empire, to understand how the impulse to violence and imperialism is central to liberal power, and how it was liberalism (informed by Orientalism), that served as a justificatory logic for much of West's colonial ventures.

In almost all the variants of secularism, the solution that secularism proffers lies not so much in tolerating difference or celebrating diversity but in remaking/constructing certain kinds of religious subjectivities and expressions (even if this requires the use of violence) so as to render them compliant with liberal political rule. So regardless of the forms of power that secularism might use, the governing logic is always the subjection of "religion" to the nation-state. Now, a nation-state might use brute violence to suppress religion (as the French/Turkish experience goes), or it might regulate religion through indifference, which is to say that it privatizes, individualizes, depoliticizes religion, and hence remakes it in very profound ways.

State is never neutral. That is a myth on which liberal nation-state stands. Instead, we can see secularism as a statist project that claims to make religious difference irrelevant to politics, while at the same time it embeds and instills majoritarian religious/ideological sensibilities and normative values in state institutions, laws, and practices (as seen in America where secularism is laced with Protestantism and in India where Hinduism and otherization of Muslims have been part of juridical frameworks since 47, long before BJP's rise to power).

Assumption that religion and politics are notions that are timelessly and universally separate, and have to distinct essences is however historically inaccurate and flawed. The notions of religion and politics are not natural or neutral. Rather, they are produced by a genealogy/historiography of secularism that gives these concepts with meaning in the first place.

To put it in simple words, before the advent of modernity, European and non-European modes of living, and especially the latter, would not be able to make any sense of such separation of the sacred and the profane.

To divorce secularism from Eurocentrism is one way of universalizing it. It is only by presenting the history of the West as the history of the world that you can do it. Secularism took different forms in different places but the impulse/logic was always rooted in certain dichotomies: public/private, religious/political, emotional/rational, legal/moral. These categories, however, are neither unquestionable, nor natural, but mere products of history that could fall apart (and do fall apart daily almost) in the real lives of people. They exist only theoretically.

The same case is made by Joseph Massad in his book, Islam in Liberalism, and Colonial Effects. We might have a utopian understanding of what liberalism is, but that is a function/effect of its hegemony and power in the world today. Domenico Losordu, in his book called Liberalism: A Counter History, shows how liberalism coexisted with racism (and justified/rationalized it), imperialism, and genocide. Instead of accepting unquestionably liberalism's story about itself, and its self-identification, you should maybe read some critiques of it and how it is built on a myth of religion's intrinsic propensity to violence, that liberalism lacks.

The underlying assumption behind attempts to equate liberalism with peace is that religion has some fanatical and dangerous proclivity to violence.

It is argued that religion spills into violence because if someone thinks that they are on a mission from God, they are not likely to participate in a communicative dialogue. However, this argument isn't really about religion but about claims that a higher/superior authority/entity is validating and condoning one's position. This higher authority, as Professor Salman Sayyid and others argue, does not have to be God, or gods. It could be Reason, Science, History.

So what liberalism does is that it hides its claims to a higher authority (as in the colonial context), while revealing the claims that people who are grounded in religion make.

Religion and politics are not two hermetically sealed off essences that you can pick up and make sense of, across time and space. Secularism is not neutral; it is always imbibed by majoritarian religious/ideological commitments.

One of the most significant ways that American society's relationship with the law has changed is due to the power of Christian religion on legislation. Despite the American Constitution's provision of the separation between church and state, Christian religion has become increasingly present, and even dominant, in the law.

As Hussein Agrama argues, one of the claims that liberalism makes is that it seeks to maintain a peaceful public order, but to maintain a peaceful public order, privileging majority's sensitivities is inevitable.

When a large part of the population views birth control with suspicion, we see them to brainless fanatics right away. Do we forget what Ughur women in China have gone through in forced sterilization camps?

What colonial settlers did to indigenous women in the USA Canada and Australia are not easily forgotten from our collective lived history.

Birth control has been used as a political tool. Controlling births is also not secular. Sex is mediated through marriage and reproduction is mediated through marriage and marriage is a social and religious institution therefore it should come as no surprise to anyone that social role play or ideas of virtue and sin predicate people's reproductive decisions .

We can't ignore or divest ourselves from these realities. We need to live in these realities to inform what a modicum and a practice needs to look like in the future.

A general aim in any law making activity that poses a moral −legal problem has been to "to refrain from imposing as law the views of any group upon another; and second, the construction of a law which would permit freedom to one group of adherents without, at the same time, violating the consciences of those who hold the opposite."

Rev. C. Sheedy, C.S.C., *Law and Morals,* **43 Chi. B. Record 375 (1962).**

The problem arises when we think only secularism can be tolerant, progressive, democratic and enlightened whereas religiously inspired ideals are essentially regressive, intolerant and undemocratic.

Making the choice for keeping the child would be easier for women, if the fathers were forced to care for the children who have had their first breath already. Also opening more shelters and homes for poor children, feeding programs, making the orphanages better, making more adoption options available are a necessary in our society. Even if you consider abortion to be a necessary evil, it's a truly upsetting thing.

It is obvious to all that religious affiliation is a fairly good predictor of voting behavior on abortion reform legislation.

The United States is a far more religious nation than Britain in terms of both church attendance and religious identification and it is hardly surprising therefore that Americans tend to take a more traditional stance on many sexual issues.

Pro-life argument also states that killing a human at any stage of is a disgrace to humanity. A fetus is the beginning of life and even after six weeks of pregnancy, a fetus has a heartbeat giving a fetus the right to life. So, abortion is considered murder and direct goes against GOD will. Irrespective of a woman's condition (poor, drunk user, or young) no one has a right to deprive a soul of entering the world.

Pro-life doctors also claim that by the end of 1st trimester whole baby is formed in the womb having eyes, hands, legs, and all body parts and just like a miniature human being. Abortion at this stage is done by breaking the whole baby and removing parts. So, it's so cruel to treat a soul this way.

Conclusion

If we decide on abortion from women it may lead to limiting their right to decide for their life and career. But on the other hand, legalizing abortion will be devaluing human life. Both sides have valid points and none can be ignored.

The current Texas Supreme Court Decision of un-legalization of abortion in Texas supports the matter of life over the matter of choice. By solving the financial issues of mothers, making better career choices possible with affordable childcare servies, and making better mental and physical health services available to women, this decision can be made acceptable and more digestible for the majority.

Some see abortion as a limitless right appropriate even as a substitute for birth control; however, others see the issue as a serious justice issue demanding we act as a voice for the voiceless.

. "A human being is a deciding being." - Viktor Frankl

Aside from the fact that, abortion is the taking of a life in most cases abortion, whether legal or illegal, is a traumatic experience thatmay have severe consequences later on.

Everyone can agree suicide is devastating and we try to prevent it, yet we still fight over what abortion really is. . Just because your opinion is that they will go nowhere in life, does not mean it is correct or true because you can't see the future. I cannot see the future therefor I prefer to take the more positive, less bitter approach that each and every child at least deserves a shot at life. What they make of that life is up to them not you- but that's what true choice means. When in both a human life is cut short and can never live to its full potential. A life under lived is distressing .People commit suicide most often for the same reason they have abortions. Pain! Some people drink to deal with the pain and some people shoot and kill to deal with the pain . Yet the pain still remains. And in turn pain begets pain.

It is time to end the pain and not the human life.

www.ingramcontent.com/pod-product-compliance
Lightning Source LLC
Chambersburg PA
CBHW052339220526
45472CB00001B/498